Drinkers Thinkers Outright Stinkers

MARK SKIRVING

The Poetic Fumblings of a Lockdown Layabout

APS PUBLICATIONS

APS Books,
The Stables Field Lane,
Aberford,
West Yorkshire
LS25 3AE

APS Books is a subsidiary of the
APS Publications imprint

www.andrewsparke.com

First published worldwide by APS Books in 2021

A catalogue record for this book is available from the British Library

ISBN 978-1-78996-510-0

Dear Reader,

This is my first collection of free verse, rhyme, anecdote, and epitaph. A right gob full. It has become a memoir of sorts composed of what I would best describe as poetic fumblings. With a backdrop of The Black Country and Brummagem, these are recollections and short glimpses into my world and the many strange chords that have been struck and have stuck.

Though not simply a poetic list of loved ones and pivotal events, many such folk and things are indeed mentioned, and I have therefore attempted some sort of chronological order. A serious bit of fun.

I hope you enjoy meeting some of the wonderfully outlandish characters that have passed through my life, together with a few equally memorable bastards.

MARK SKIRVING

A lifetime of love, fun, friendship and joie de vivre
To all who were there
Especially those who have since left us
I raise a glass xx

CONTENTS

Dangerfield Lane

Nan & Grandad's crusty cobs of haslet
Yellow haddock, luminous
And coffee in turbaned bottle camp
The smell of window seat geraniums
Battle cushions soaked, pumped oozed
Sodden
In a lifetime of farts and snoozes.
Grandad whistles well
As does the kettle
An art lost to his generation
Together with queuing, wearing hats and eating offal
A generation born and reared
Without possession
Their inescapable obsession
To cover every inch with all they possess
No surface free and left to breath
For fear the gaps may be contagious
And poverty return.
A world of Cladded
Chaos and clutter
Clogged
With mantelpiece mementos
Nick knacks and tick tocks
Decanters and doilies
A duster's nightmare
And yet
They take great care
Keeping all as spotless
As their character and kind hearts

Telly Ho!

The TV wakes with them
Spills out, throughout
It's non discerning anywhat
Volumed megawatt of aging ears
The ATV years
Our lunchtime favourites
Mr & Mrs, cosy smiles and nicities
Paint Along with Nancy Kiminski's daubs of still life
All palette knife purples, pap and orange slap
And then a TV gap
Afternoon nap
'Til Teatime chimes
And The Crossroads Motel calls out it's guitar twang
Sandy and Meg
Miss Diane and the longing pudgy face of Benny
His soft ways and wellies
Dipped in shit
Serve as a reminder
Young Sir!
Prepare!
Uncle Paul's throne of 'Express & Star'
So that we may protect Nan's cushions
From the smelting filth of hard graft
As he chomps his egg and beans
Bostin'!

The Lure of the Bureau Drawer

Permission to mooch?
Permission denied
But why? I cried
Come out of there
What have we told you?
Where, stretched to fullest
Toe tip reach
Little fingers bled
Tears were shed
A razor blade blindly fingered
So now
I sneak
Seek
Safety atop Nan's black leather foot pouffe
Have a proper look see
In awe
The lure of the bureau drawer
It's earthly delights
This Aladdin's man cave of over spill
A peerless assemblage of superfluous and curio
So much
Redundant such and such
And the like
Bottle opener and smelling salts
Eye bath and rubber thimble
Poker dice and a magnet
Old foreign coins with polo mint holes
Buttoneer
Trim Comb
All things Ronco
No 'Rhinestone Stud Setter' mind
I'm sad to find
Best make do with one shake of the snow globe and I'm out of here!
Bloomin' Ada
Just a tick, quick!
I've found a small mirror
On a telescopic stick.

Father Christmas 1970

Bent over the settee
With cheeks open wide
I cannot hide
My 'Tiny Tears' of shame.
Through cushion muffled cries
My Father
Eyes and dutifully tries
To push
Digit prod
A suppository up my unyielding Harris
For a second time
Post first refusal
Pop out, shot out
What's it all about?
Alfie!
All this
Under the ever present eye of Father Christmas.
Too much to bear
Buttocks!
His festive stare
That clocks my every move of every day
Passing judgement Christmas Eve
On what I am about to receive
Hell
Would you believe
The boy next door is watched by Jesus
Christ!
Thank God my Dad won't have his bloody nonsense in our house
It's left to Father Christmas to tot up my doings
The cheers and the booings
Like chasing the cat with a stick
Flick.
We once caught a train to his place
This old Saint Nick
Met face to face
Where perched upon his knee
I unwrapped a handbag!

And gave him in return
Enough tears to fill it
Oh no, please no
No Ho Ho Ho
'Til Mother's whispers saw it swapped
Tears stopped
For a plastic telescope
A proper lads toy
This pretty boy
Best 'get his bloody hair cut' as Grandad says.
Anyways...
I thought he lived at The North Pole
Now don't tell a living soul
But he stays at John Lewis' in Brum.
There's no Reindeer or elves
Just bottles on shelves
And nice smelling ladies
With made up faces like Charlie Cairoli.
They sprayed my mom's wrist with a nice whiff
We both took a sniff
Mmmmmm 'Old man's arsehole' as Roy's Nan always says
Christmas holidays…
Smashin'.

Double Agent

My Mom and Dad are splitting up, I cry and wet the bed
Age nine, I cannot comprehend what new life lies ahead

Pretty soon I realise I've twice the stuff to do
My double life brings twice the craic and other halves anew

Trevor, Mother's husband and Bridget, Father's wife
A cloud with silver lining brought two new dear friends for life

Into The Pantry

Into the pantry go I
I may be gone for some time
Access granted and gained
Intentions feigned
The pretence?
A mere two biscuit expedition
The cheap grey cardboard ones that taste of nothing.
As the door closes behind me
Out of sight
My eyes refocus
Acclimatize to the lack of light
I've only a matter of two minutes
Possibly three
To silently slice and scoff
Oh my!
The largest wedge of pork pie
The clock is ticking
I chomp down five large, pickled onions
Strong and malted mind
And then to find
Maybe too, just a handful of those sweetest little silver skins
Yum
Job done
I step out from the darkness
To a hero's welcome
I smile and the room smiles back
I have two strips of cardboard to dip in my three sugars minimum
I've fooled them again
Haven't I?

The Sorcerer's Apprentice

First year school juniors
Assembly Hall sing along
A piano duet
Play hymns to forget
'All things bored but dutiful'
We sit
Legs crossed
Lost
In our prods and whispers
Then WOOSH!
A four fisted roll of notes comes straight at me
Rollicking thunder
Twists of whitewater
Burns and brands
Deep
My tender young spirit
A mischievous magic
Woven
Into one euphoric pulse of rhythm
My convulsions
Burst unmuzzled
An eruption of helpless laughter
Pure and sinful
Pure and simple
Joy.
Whilst the current drifts by
All other ears
Unfathomably
Unnoticed
The sorcery has found it's apprentice
Hit it's Mark.
My path is laid there and then
A moment in time
To define
The rest of my life.
Appetite wet, course set
A train ride chug a rhythm of Boogie Woogie.

My 10 Year Old Twitch

Panties pulled
From fanny bald
Knock knees spread wide
She stands and piss streamed down the slide
Where waiting, I stand
In open gawp
Poking and thwacking with my best stick
The oncoming yellow widdle relief
My first such sighting
Exciting, inviting
The second would follow within minutes
As would the third.
My interest noted
I'm offered two for the price of none
Come on!
A private viewing of privates
To commence with eager imminence.
Together, she, her friend and me
Enter our makeshift Moulin Rouge
And there
Without a care
In Anderson Shelter dim lit dank
Cheesy 'Whatsits' stank
Skirts were held high with knickers down
They put on their little show
Give my ten year old self a giggle tease glimpse of future excitements
With a deep belly oddness
And a full twitch of the tiddler
I thanked Jesus
Though I don't know why.

The Golden Shot

In the Park Keeper's pockets
I think you'll find
Women's knickers pinched off the line
Whilst Clemmy's cardigans left behind
Dirty bloody bugger!
He now stands within range
Wire fence fixing
Forward tilting
Reveals expanse of fat back and arse crack
Target of the day.
Me?
Peeping from curtained window of stifled giggles
Gat gun ready
Steady
Pull!
With dog like yelp
He springs attention
Drops his pliers to the floor.
I will wait
Ten minutes ticking
For lowered guard complacency
And repeat!
Yelp!
Sweet!

Orange Chips

Orange chips and batter bits
Bag or cone or posh on plate
Any salt and vinegar love?
Loads of both, that's bloomin' great

Look Ma, I'm On Top Of The World

'Hey Johnny, gonna stick it to ya see'
Little Caesar's Edward G
Scarface wannabe
You talkin' to me?
Make your move shit heal
Ron & Reggie's legacy.
I'm an air pistol packer Pellet popper
You'll never take me alive Copper
Mess with me and come a cropper.
Nicked from Dad's cupboard and ready to fire
12 year old Gun for hire
Tin can Hit man Rarin' to go
Shot a park keeper's arse you know
And now my first Scout
But as I shoot he moves about
Shouts out
I've nicked his cheek
It begins to leak
Shit, shit, shit
I didn't mean to hit him in the face
Panic, Run, A hiding place?
Darlo flats
Straight up the staircase to the very top
A sniper's last stop
A Cop car skids up
And up the stairwell they run
No time to hide my gun
Gotcha ya little shit
You're under arrest
Driven to the station where all's confessed
I give them a number to phone
Easy touch, Nan Joan
Don't tell Mom or Dad
Pleads me
Weepily

But, they will know
My cheeks will glow
And then my day in court
Lesson taught
12 months conditional discharge
I'm back at large
Still a play up prankster
But gangster?
Nah
Mafioso no go
When the going gets tough
They don't call their Nans.

Uncle Eric

Handsome devil was Uncle Eric
They say a poor man's Errol Flynn
Quick to rile with knockout punch
'Til TB got the best of him.

'Great Uncle Len

Skipping prancer, Muppet dancer
Half a bitter whistle wets
Nosferatu on the dance floor
Plays imagined castanets
Full of self and pin striped posture
Nan had measure of the mon
Clout bang hit across his forehead
Nearly broke her frying pon.

Single Parent Child

Single parent child
That's me
Yippee!
Entitled to a free uniform from Fossbrook's
Frankenstein monstrous
'You'll grow into it'
'You're on benefit'
Free school dinners
Means back of the queue. Fuck you!
Fuck you too!
Plumbum Pendulitis, I'm off!
Can't stigmatize me
Pence fiddled free
From slot of Mother's telephone piggy wiggy
And now exchanged for orange chips and batter bits
My Black Country escape.
Two fat ladies, Nora and Dora
Faces flush and fryers at full sizzle
Bingo wings at full swing
Shovel, wrap and box up
Endless orders from huge foundry men with minstrel faces
Taking their lunch break from back break
And the mighty drop hammers that forge steal
Gaining strength from their Vulcan fire God
Ground shaking metronome
Pound, Pound, Pound.
Pounding out it's dance of sweat and flying spark
Flickering in the dirt track darkness
Of red diesel's hidden secret knowings
Comings and goings. Gone.
Little did I realize I was witnessing it's last
It's day already passed
'I remember when this was all fields'
Said my Grandparents, pointing at factories.
'I remember when this was all factories'
Now says me, pointing at fields.

Peasant

'Well, are you a peasant Boy?'
Hisses the beak of old Mr Pingu
Rocking on the balls of his fig roll shod feet
Pocketed fists almost squeak
Clench and release
Anus like
His ill fitted jacket tugged toward crotch
Raising arse flap to full mast
Bitter tongue tip
Poking in and out
His bubbling trap
Like a dog's lipstick
A beetle like sucking frenzy
On a lump of shit
Gasping for air
Rasping for air
Breathless with the giddy excitement
Of bullying
A twelve year old boy
The sea spray delight
Foams the corners of his sneer
Like a spunk trumpet's fanfare
'No Sir' wept the boy in anger
But, in all honesty…

Poor Dog

Poor Dog shut in a flat
Nothing to do
But chew and shit and shit and chew
Slop turd minefield
In puddles of piss
For me to miss
Tread carefully kid
But always caught by morning's daze
One small step for man
Transferred weight, too late
Warm shit stink
Oozes up between my toes
Mom! That fuckin' Dog I wish it would die
But Mom's in bed
Just gives a sigh
Poor Dog shut in a flat
Nothing to do
But chew and shit and shit and chew
All that pocket money saved
Gnawed and pawed beyond saving
My Fonz leather jacket
Well plastic
Waist and cuffs of elastic
Chewed and spewed
The pieces lay
Strewn along the hallway
Pieces of me
I wanted you to see
The me
I was desperate to be
Oh NO!
Not my black suede Winkle Picker Boots
MOM! That fuckin' Dog
I wish it would die
And now when I look back
And think of that poor fuckin' Dog
I want to cry

Mr Oi Shutup Can Yow

Mr Oi Shutup Can Yow
Ran out of sticks of chalk to throw
The Maths would wait, equations held
It's time a cheeky boy was felled
Boys held down, pressed to the floor
'Til twisted arms can take no more
Some hopelessly retaliate
But most just cry, accept their fate
Bruises, nosebleeds, tears of woe
That's Mr Oi Shutup Can Yow

Me and Mr D

Aged fourteen we climbed a crane
And took six cans of Special Brew
Once drunk we looked back down to Earth
And wondered what the fuck to do

Kinky Bob

All polished boots and Burton suits
A proper ten bob millionaire
Kinky Bobby raised his comb
And all of Walsall stopped to stare

Open mouthed, with bated breath
Each and every watched in awe
As Curtis quiff, unnatural stiff
Did slip from perch and drop to floor

The '78 Comeback Special

The Hillbilly Cat
The Undisputed, Tutti Fruited
King of Rock a Hula
Bop n Roll
Lip curled sneer and leer
Quiff teased and collars hoisted
Heavenward
50,000,000 fans can't be wrong
Drops on The Ferguson
Begins to spin, Full din
All the big knobs
Bass And Treble
Fuck me Wednesbury
We're off!
Pelvic gyration, Bobby Soxer adulation
Though the mirror shows nothing from the waist down
Teeny Boppers scream and screech, Reach
Out to touch
'Thank you very much'
Fringed cowpoke shirt
Black jeans and orange carpet slippers
Wear thin the rug
With a frenzy of bopped up static
Seizure and spasm
Electrified coiffure and sideburn prepubescent wisps
A lung full of Presley
Hollers, Caterwauls
Into mop handle microphone
It's a one for the money, honey
All my best moves
Rock a billy grooves
And Go cat go
Scotty takes a solo
The neighbour bangs on her ceiling
From the flat below
I've got to go, Old witch
I've got stitch anyway!

Over my shoulder
One last smoulder
A parting salute to the mirror and adiós amigos
Elvis has left the living room
Thank you
And goodnight.

The Redmaster

You there, Stand up boy
Teacher, leecher
Supposed Pillar of the community
Fiery ill tempered
Purple faced bluster
Honestly Sir, it wasn't me
A fine example he turned out to be
A man made for stocks and all the town to gather
Face like a tomato that's already been thrown at himself
Sir
You've let yourself down
You've let your parents down
You let the school down
Red face got caught red faced, red handed
Hand in the till, creaming off his fill
No blood pressure pill
Can save him now
Nick name earned
Sir
Stand at the blackboard with your nose
Pressed against the chalk mark
So we don't have to look at your
Stupid
Red
Face

Cook Street

Old Dora Dyke picks up a broom
And swings it like a dream
With a scream
Of 'Trollop'
Wallop!
Brushes me from her back yard's shite house.
Bad news!
My 'Brothel Creeper' shoes
Are found most unwelcome
And guilty by association
I receive the full force of besom bristle
Dismissal
'Compo' to her 'Nora'
Nemesis!
I'm swept off the premises
But not before I catch a glimpse of what lies within.
'The Monster' Nicholas
Sits wrapped in an army surplus blanket
His gurning face
Sits in place
Six inches from the telly box
Helplessly tittering and Wittering
The Great Big
Biker
Outlaw
Bastard!
We will return at 4am
To knock upon his sleepy door
And pelt him with bricks
Give him what for
And then?

Run like fuck!

Wish us luck, we'll need it!

The Ballad of Cut Throat H

Tank full of terter werter
Honda 50 revved to rock
Cut Throat H with razor holstered
Takes a spin around the block

Throttle full, he reaches 30
Leathers glint in Summer sun
But Mom is waiting on the doorstep
Get in Alan, your tea is done

The Organist Entertains

Pumped full of himself
To bursting and beyond palatable
He floats balloon, rasp, fart around the ceiling
To sniff at Sodom's portals
Pudgy wrists of bangled hoopla
Dripping gold and Brandy chasers
Sticky fat touch stubs of sweaty soft cheese
Tit fingering at his keys Wurlitzer
Double manual and pedals
Una paloma blanca
Pump shiter
The wearer of long white stockings no doubt
White like his name
Not blue like his bitchy mouth

The Singing Brickie

Georgie White, the singing brickie
Ate whole chickens, bones and all
His hands so strong could crush a spud
His shoulders wide as he was tall

He chewed on lightbulbs, swallowed glass
A raw egg eating record holder
Sang his heart out every day
With hod of bricks upon his shoulder

Building sites to market squares
Light operatics of your choice
A human jukebox of the classics
With his velvet tenor voice

He played 'The last post' on the bugle
Respect shown at the cenotaph
Always tipped his hat to ladies
A nod and wink to make them laugh

George found time for everyone
Was stopped for handshakes in the street
A few more steps then stopped again
His endless days of 'meet and greet'

He knew all and all new him
His stocky frame stood out a mile
He lived it large, stood loud and proud
And every bit with old school style.

Darlo School Leaver '82

From the great high rises
They drop like flieses
Passing the heavy baton of hopelessness and tears
To the next mon
Who shovels them up from the pavement
To then make his own climb
Reach the rooftops of despair
And there
Does prepare
To make his own jump
THUMP!
A proud people aren't sure
What to be proud of any more
There are no bread winners here
Only losers
Week day boozers
Work has long ceased and become nothing more than a story
Passed down from Father to Son
'You could walk out of one job in the morning and walk into another
by the afternoon!'
Even the three day week seems like '70's chic.
Men have no manly things to do
But lash out and fight amongst themselves
Factories and foundries?
Gone
A mon
Must make sweat in the gym.
I love Darlo
But time to go
So plan my great escape
Music will dig my tunnel out
And a billion grains of imagination will be the sand hidden in my
turn ups.

Haircut Harris

His moniker earned
When Land Rover upturned
Sliced the top
Boiled egg and soldiers
Straight off his skull.
Trepanning
With no forward planning
The skilled hands of Dr Merriweather
Saw his nut pieced back together
Like an archaeological pot.
Riveted
Reconnected
Metal detected
With a strong band of steal
It would slowly heal
With a circular parting permanent.
A hairstyle of two levels
Upper and lower
In between?
A no grower.
When Haircut Harris came to town
Kids would follow him around
He'd hand out magnets
For them to place about his noggin.
Our Six million dollar man
Not faster, not stronger
Just a cranium
That little bit longer
And a halo of magnets to boot.

Shakey Bill

His Chinese hair came Aloha from Hawaii Via Satellite
A dyed black budgie cage
With stirrups
Perhaps a miner's canary
Fart catcher
Visibly perched within
An odd hat, sat
Unnatural habitat
Upon aging pale brow and pink eyelids
His Hubba Bubba chewin' chops
Bubble face pops
And tits clap along to the tune
Of Pat Boone
Glory Hallelujah!
It'll be over soon
The Dance of the 6-inch turnups

Only The Lonely

When someone you love says goodbye
All their faults evaporate
Leaving only your own
To mull over and regret
And wonder why

The Woodpile

'Scuse me mate, but where's The Woodpile
Must be somewhere off this street?'
'Don't go looking there my friend
I tell you they eat Human meat!'

A Bit Of An Accident

'Mrs Harper's had a bit of an accident with some timber'
Said the German Expressionist Happening
Known as Eric.
His long cadaverous
Stink fingers Stroke
Sgt. Wilson like
Across a vast brow
Of feigned concern
And furtive glances.
To wit
Blood speckled spectacles
Sit
Split
In two
Amid dubious porcelains
Upon the mantle shelf.
'An accident'
Fizzzzzzzzzzzzzzz lisped his echoing wife
Jill
Her face of sticking plaster
Matrimonial disaster
Splintered and teary eyed
Where said spectacles once rested.
With gross misjudgement
She'd entered the sanctum of potting shed
Cross pollination disruption
Eruption
Divine retribution
Meted
In a Holy instant.
THUD!
A length of two by four
Made so very sure
It was a mistake she would not repeat.
Her slow-witted face, torn and blackened.
Her hair containing the odd oat
Of upturned porridge bowl not two weeks passed.

A poor sad Hermintrude
Who's teats were never milked.
And lost her bite
To the thrust of a broom handle
Oh Jill, Jill
If only you had stayed up that hill
And not soiled your pale.

A New Bench

They've got a new bench in the park Sid
Just here, across the way
My Grandad looked, then looked again
As something felt astray

It looks a lot like our bench Jess
Said Grandad to my Nan
I must confess, it does said Jess
And out the back they ran

It is our bloody bench Sid
It bloody is an' all
And now I've swore. And so have I
Best go and fetch our Paul

Well Uncle Paul and Grandad Sid
Went out and fetched the bench
Returned it to it's rightful place
Whilst pardoning their French

Well just what kind of silly sod
Would play a prank like that?
Then penny dropped, the pointing stopped
Best get my coat and hat

Harper's Bizarre

I lob my Wing Wah Ahhhh
Eric turns A moment
Turner Prize
Long Grain Silhouetted
Upon the kitchen door
A number 94, Special fried rice
He lunges in hot pursuit.
I lead for two laps of the three-seater divan
Catch me if you can
Before upturning him over back of said
Upon his Christopher Wren
Domed head
I've fled
Whilst he ungainly lies
Arse over tit
I leave by the front door
In a gentlemanly fashion.
'I'd rather burn the Bible than have that filthy fucker in my house',
Shouts Eric
My ticket earned
All boats burned
And yet
With bad wig and snorkel jacket
My new alias of Simple Tony
Sees me welcomed
Once more across his threshold.
But behold!
One night, a second Tony, Double phoney
Turns up
And though confusion and visible bafflement ensues
There comes acceptance
Upon the settee
Sits Tony Two, Eric and Tony Me
Symmetry.

Agent Orange

Mutha will never suspect
[Incorrect!]
I have her pump action garden hose
And by Gawd it goes
Everywhere
With me on the bus
As does Mr Prince
A water diviner of some skill and eminence
About the lower deck
He slowly paces
Captivated nay apprehensive faces
Hovers, Twitches
His forked dowsing stick
Works its magic trick
Witching rod of hazel
Picks out the puddles I'm about to make
And take
No prisoners
The legacy of Barney McGrew
Blow holes forth
Adjusted nozzle to maximum coverage
Pressured fury
Of hose and passengers alike
Steaming Screaming
Much commotion
From those who thought to travel dry today
But hey hey.
Empty!
We face a seething sea
Best head back to shore
Slowly back our way towards the door
A full gallon lighter
Our spot could not be tighter
Thank you, driver,
I really think this is our stop.

Portobello

High rise flats and homemade tatts
Necks, knuckles, oversized belt buckles
Scrawl, dots and borstal spots
Forearms for special Moms and lists of unwanted kids
[to remember their Birthdays].
It took Maureen Derby three days to find the turd I left in her bed
Dirty bitch. Nuff said! [I hid twenty bottles of milk in her settee].
Can you smell fish?
It ain't me. I had a bath before I came out.
What stinks of piss and doesn't work?
The lifts, the phone box, the residence
All under the watchful eye of
Local copper in a cape
In a cape, I do not jape, I bet he's got a whistle
In his titted bonce perhaps
A Bobby of the Silver Screen
Waves a lantern in the fog
Through shadowed screams and clip clop
Anyway, I digress, back to…
Tess and her brown paper bag tits
Not fit for Morecambe's magic
Screams through her Bells blended stink
Jim, Jim, ya big dicked fuckin' bastard
Get them Feathers out a here.
Her weekend specials
Of shimmering sky blue spandex
Pulled taught
On her Wolverhampton Wanderers
Legs bowed like a magnet
But without the pulling power
The last decade of thin poor people
Not fat as fuck like now
Got any tattoos mate?
No.
Why not?
?

Glue

We had our laughs
Back of Darlo Baths
Brought Woodpile madness, badness and sin
In a stolen tin
Of adolescent misuse
Solvent abuse and who gives a fuck
Rogues and misfits
Comprehensive school's nobody's fools
But our own
Choice!
Fireside friendships, gathered 'round flame
Ceremonial circle of The Ancients
Vodka, Vimto and J.P.S.
The pop, snap, crackle
And wood whistle fizz
The gunshot and whizzbang
Of asbestos, tossed
Into the blaze
We blankly gaze
And puff and push
On loaded sniff bags
Our slow motion faces
Heavy in snot
And glue blackened sticky
Contortion Distortion
Gurn our way into oblivion
45's played at 33
A new reality
Percy Pliers dentistry
Clamps upon our teeth
In lock jawed grip
Don't flip
Enjoy the trip
The Evostick kick of the day

Johnny Satan's Sideburns

Johnny Satan's giant sideburns
Overwhelmed his titchy face
Fought for space
Satan's speciality statement pieces
70's Ted head, facial props,
Novelty mutton chops
Unnaturally black as a coal man's sack
And as black as the mail we're about to send him
By happy chance
We'd happen to glance
At the not so private lives
Gynaecological presentations within Reader's Wives
The chopped liver special
And there for all to see
Miss Gristle of '83
Was Satan's Missus like spring bow dividers
Not one for the neighbours I'll bet
And there lay the threat
We knew exactly what to get
With cut out letters and retype set
Correct ransom note etiquette
Took our stand
Made our postal demands
His whiskers to be sheared, cleared
And placed in the envelope provided
Covertly left where his privet divided
And there make our fair and hairy exchange
Happy Days!
He's never liked our youthful ways
Always sneers and says
'Bloody Philistines!'

Half A Head Tony Baloney

Half a Head Tony
Had a full face below the trilby
But very little within the hat itself.
On untitfered days he made an excellent bird bath
And folk would try not to stare
At what blatantly wasn't there.
Having little crown to find purchase
A full head of hair
Now infested his snotter.
It spat from drinkers beak with re channelled vigour
Sitting heavily rusted
Atop his hip flask grin
Recorded message played within
'Is it yow or yower kid?'
He'd always say.
Chuckle, pass the time of day.
Then reload,
Return to standby mode
Until our next encounter.
'Is it yow or yower kid?'
Again he'd say.
Chuckle, pass the time of day.
Then reload,
Return to standby mode
Until our next encounter.'Is it …
Mmmm, I wonder which came first?
The question or the head?

Smokey and The Bandits

Wincanton lorry park
A right lark after dark
Cheekily, sneakily
Handles quietly tried and tested
For open sesame
And sweet success Yes!
What a score!
The Great Pie Robbers of '84
Eight tonnes of Melton Mowbray's finest
Will come along for the ride
We climb inside
Keys in the cab Result!
And the plan?
To crash the security barrier and drive full throttle until the end of
time. Become as legendary as the Brooksy mob
Who stole the 339 bus!
Why?
Because!!
We're on a mission - Ignition!
Mr Dyke at the wheel
The Musketeers
Mr Jones and myself
We give three cheers
All for one and one for all
As a torch light appears
Shit!
Foot to the floor
Shit!
Stop the clock A steering lock
Navigation limitation Forward or reverse
Shit!
Houston
We have a ... LIFT OFF!
Touched cloth
Beast unleashed
Straight through 8ft of steal fence it lunges
And plunges into a ditch

Slight glitch
We bale out and try to scramble
But for an entanglement of barbed wire
Remove attire
Torn and tattered but free
Run for liberty
Lost to the night
We live to fight
Another day
Another story
And just a little Small town glory

Noose Lane Riffs

I took the kicking of my life
Heard one shout stick in the knife
In blooded ball I lay in fear
But my mate's courage means I'm still here

Night Of The Living Dead

Our rise and fall was very small.
A short lived four gig frenzy of blood, guts and banishment
Unleash the Hogwurst
Slaughter house party trimmings
And abattoir Ha Ha
Hors d'oeuvre s and spray of the day
Anyone for a bag of lungs?
This blooded pork and hog harvest
Propelled amongst the crowd
Pigs heads launched and giblets flung
Bullseye
'Cut Throat H', heavily felled
Drops unconscious
His ginger quiff and armpits
Takes the blow
Will miss the show
And on we merrily go
Heavy bass rumble of the Zorch men's approach
Approaching danger.
Stop.
Bollocks, I've dropped my plectrum.
I turn and bend over.
Cut away jeans
Bare arse and plums
Plectrum retrieved
Approaching danger resumes
With lightning crack snare and Thor's mighty thunder thrashed
'Brada' pummels and pounds
Up notches to ramming speed
And a bit!
Stratocastic stabs, scream out the devil's licks of 'Jones' sadistic fingers
Pressed upon the throats of strangers
Step forth The Nazarine
Tipton Slasher
Monster Masher
A blade waving Pagey swoops down from the rooftops
And howls to Moon The Loon

Awake my old Darling Darlo and rise from your sleepy slow death
We up the ante
And proudly present
Kick, pout, thrust, block
Our Lesbian karate formation team
Pace the floor, no punches pulled
Amongst the bods
Punks and Teds and Skins and Mods
Family, Friends and a few Bellends
All have paid their 60p
To come see
Our Pistol Presley of adolescent mutation and hormonal rutting
We ride our musical ghost train guffaws
To amplified insanity
Arthur Askey's hearing aid
Lies blood soaked upon the parquet flooring
Worst fears and too late tears
Of caretakers, promoters and club entertainment secretaries
Who's bleedin' idea was this lot?
You're barred, banned for life, if you ever come back we'll call the
police.
Comic Punksters, chances took
Foundations shook and ceremonially shat on
Darlo Town Hall received it's rude awakening
Only to hit the snooze button and nod back off for the next forty years

Time for a comeback me thinks
Bollocks, I've dropped my plectrum again.

Hail, Hail Rock n Roll

Just how many
Took or lost their cherry
To the sounds of Mr Berry
The birth of a music
The conceivement of a generation
Gave a voice to teenage dreams
Of engine rumblings
And youthful fumblings
Through wit and wink
Brought eight to the bar
To a six string guitar
And duck walked his way
Into Rock 'n' Roll Glory

Farewell tenor sax
The young buck of Jazz
Who smooched and sleazed
Took flights of euphoria
Thought you were here to stay
As you growled and screamed
Your way
Had your Rock 'n' Roll heyday
From bad lad to Grandad
The Honkers and Bar walkers
Once rockin' Pied Pipers
Fade from the spotlight
The changing of the guard
Chess
Yes
Gibson Sunburst
Takes Selmer Mk.6
Chuck mate!

The Saddlers Centre – Security Skirving

Walkie Talkie Disconcerting
Most unnerving
'Security Skirving!
Please proceed immediately to Don Miller's Hot Bread Kitchen.
Migsa is mounting the counter.........over!'
The Scourge of Walsall's
Tavern in the Town
Something from the dark ages
Best kept in cages
The face of a thousand glassings, given and received
Framed in an ill-fitting 'Calm Down'
Perm and moustache.
He has known many a truncheon
Used in vain
He feels no pain
A criminally insane
Heavily graffitied street shouter and clouter
Rib breaker and widow maker of some standing
The Bogey Man.
I can only envisage my own death
And with a deep breathe
Slowly walk towards my fate, Wait!
Very slowly!
Past 'Chelsea Girl' and 'Tandy'
I nervously whistle a tune
The theme from 'High Noon'
'Do not forsake me oh my......'
Why?
Did I don the sheriff's badge?
A most reluctant moth to the flame
I suddenly hear my name!
'Security Skirving
Stand down.
Migsa has left the centre, over.'
I let out a huge sigh
Today will not be the day that I die.
Just a few scattered ice buns and a lone scotch pie.

Mr Cockle

Somewhere hidden
Forbidden
Beyond the great glory day gates
Of Old Patent Shaft Steal Works
Lies The Cockle man graveyard
A thousand wicker baskets strewn.
Lost, beneath bramble
Entangle
And rusty sheets of corrugated iron
Those distant slurred memories
Of our white jacket hero
Salivation creation
Gastropod gastronomy
His sea sluggery selection
Post 10 pint digestif perfection
We grazed upon his tubs and trays
With cocktail sticks
A bivalve mollusc pick and mix
Shelled winkle stinks
And lightly peppered keel haulers
Packets of pink titches
Barnacle Billy Boys and Molly Maloners
All wet about the ears, with a Sarson's splash
Pub to club
He cuts a fine dash
Fine dining table service
From one to the next
Glides Mr Cockle
Bringing tastes of the sea
To The Black Country we
Then off
Across the lightly saw dusted dance floor
Voyage Bon! And gone, forever more
Adead Adead O

Mick The Barber

Mirror mirror on the wall
Cracked as fuck and Brylcream smeared
Rests upon an unplumbed sink
Where nub ends sit with bits of beard

'Short back and sides, or full Duck's Arse?'
Either way you get the same
Shaking like a shitting dog
Mick lifts the scissors and takes aim

The Gents is just a cellar door
Open, stand and take a slash
Don't breathe in and jerk away
Or passers by will get a flash

Each haircut equals Barley Wine
So once you're done Mick shuts the shop
Up and down the pub and back
To earn enough for his next drop

Midnight Caller

Tap at the window, Clink of the bottles
Asti spew fizz, is held up to view
The Captain is calling, on my dear Mother
Full blazer and flannels, his mission to woo

Decisions, decisions, a yay or a nay
She keeps the chap guessing, a few minutes more
The curtains get drawn, I'm afraid it's a no no
For future attempts, best make two bottles four!

Mad Uncle Brian

Canon mouthed muck savage, engineer most sort
Bursting with rant and ruddy faced laughs guffaw
Can hold no longer, excitable trap of frothing spittle
His boiling over pasta pan
Dripped and wiped from vulgar chin
Springs to foot, bolt up attention
Makes his declaration
'I fuckin' love this cunt'
Bellowed out to pin drop stand still
'Language!'
Plants my cheek a kiss of beer dipped ginger bristle
Hugs me, squeezes me and calls me George
'I fuckin' love this cunt'
'Sit down, or I'll have to ask you to leave'
'Sinatra!'
'Pardon'
'Dean Martin!'
He likes to shout out the crooners
'Shut the fuck up
I'm trying to make a speech at my Mother's wedding'
Brian roars with snotted laughter
Works his way through the Rat Pack
'Sammy Davis'
'Shut the fucking fuck up you cunt'
He bangs the table ape like excitement
Squeals in stuck pig fashion
It's all too much
His cancerous bowel
For which he chose no treatment
Makes movement, foul
The air fills with unmistakable
Shit and blood
'Please raise your glasses
I give you - The Bride and Groom'

'SAMMY FUCKIN DAVIS!'

Monkey Mick's Cider House

Grand opening day at Monkey Mick's
I drank nine pints at nine percent
Lumpy scrumpy on the house
O'Neill was always such a gent

The finest Somerset had to offer
Handpicked and supped by Mick himself
None can leave 'til bar drunk dry
So raise a glass and drink your health

Escape committees formed and floundered
Ordered cabs sent on their way
Families left to wait and wonder
Many lost their jobs that day

I myself got home at midnight
Wanda stared me in the eye
I stood and pissed on bedroom carpet
And waved our relationship goodbye

Sad, Mad Pad

Sad, Mad Pad
Hung himself
Could not feel the love nor hope
He teetered on that stool for twenty years
Found peace at the end of a rope

The Day the Dick Went Bang

Service station anticipation
Roll up, roll up, for sideshow delight
In gentlemen's convenience, let's take a look see
Gawp at disfigurement, Behold the sight

A full hand cradles and frees from taught trouser
All bloated and blooded of purple and black
Like a well-seasoned haggis kicked twice 'round the carpark
More ballcock than cock, we're taken aback

Stretched to tearful and scarily then some
Verging on split burst, ready to pop
This offal bag piss leaker, brings on the laughter
The screams and hysterics seemed never to stop

The glory of gory and others misfortune
We stamped and we shouted, elated we sang
And all who were there would forever remember
That fateful day the dick went bang

Tunner Wiffnall's Whiff

Fuck me, did you smell his breath
He's ate a bowl of Shit & Sugar
Finally, when his teeth dropped out
'Twas safe to turn and face the bugger

Burnt Dave

Burnt Dave drops
Belly flops from pub doorway
Fuckwittedly full
Of top shelf
'Too your health'
A toddlers lurch
Forward!
Jazz hands
The full 'Mammy'
He staggers and stumble bumps
The wall clutching length of Ivy Rd
An Alpine like accent and decent
Of a slack stringed puppet
His brave peregrinations
Bobbing without guide rope or special needs helmet
Back to The President's Guest House
He will rest his charred head until the crack of eggs and bacon
Serve toast with a shaky mitt
And wish his guests a fine morning
Before taking his constitutional
Back to tipple whence he came
More of the same
Pints and chasers
Repeats until death.

Terry The Toupé

In his orange hat, he sat
Arms of artexing steal, behind the wheel
Of 150 quids worth of next week's tat
Unlicensed chancer, teddy bop dancer
'Steve, where's me frickin' dancin' shoes'
Beautifully pressed, shirt on barrel chest
Tiny legs splayed Chaplin like
Tippy toe dipped in white plimsoll
'Are you happy, Happy?'
Dancefloor Terminator, spin ladies spin
Thrown, twirled and flipped, jived two at a time
Happy to give them a dance and a drink
But not the other,'their holes frickin' stink'
'What would I want with a woman at my my age?
I can iron me own frickin' shirts.
Ooh sorry your highness!'
Lion heart of gold, loyal, fearless, friend to all
Though!
Formidable foe, to those who know
Too late, make, their biggest mistake
Inhuman strength and rage
Nurtured at the end of his father's snooker cue
Malaysian jungle fighter,
Antipodean pile driver
Used to work with Mickey Rooney's son
'Cried like a little baby, the bastard.'
Bouncers, boxers, pistoleros and jousters
Beer swilling boasters and have a go jokers
All comers welcome, to lift his lid
Hay makers for piss takers,
BOOM......
Once the syrup goes up, they go down
Lie wallop fucked
In a puddle of blooded regret
Face and fist collide
Jaw unhinged on one side
A gobshite's smile

Lies on the car park floor
Like ancient runes to be read
'Don't do it' they said
'Nobody takes Terry Brown for a cunt.
Scratch! I'll have a pint of Brown & Mild mate.'

Mr Mitten

Scruff necked and ticketed
Tossed arse over tit from each and every
Charlie 'Bad Boy' 'Blues Boy' Mitten
Lies slumber fucked
At the bottom of the stairs he's just been thrown down
His obnoxicated dribble tongue still whispers shit
His crotch seeps the 'Harvey's Bristol' of previous
Soaked in sozzle, then white spirit rinsed
Hands that once fingerpicked 'The Blues'
Now clutch at the pavement with familiarity
The daydreams of Parisian nights
Busking with Wreckless Eric and writing 'The Novel'
Spill out into the gutter
Leaving a cleansed and empty head
Gurgling from the grin of fools.
Passing trade
Made to step over him
'Hello Charlie', some pay their respects
Charlie 'Bad Boy' 'Blues Boy' Mitten
Lies there
Dead drunk.
Dead

Where's Your Boots Superman?

German girlfriend
Fraulein Roundthebend
Besotted with Superman
So how to match up?
'Why must you English all have such bad teeth?'
Well?
What the Arian hell
As snow fell
With fancy hired secret , tucked beneath Winter's wool
We set upon our weekly shop
Once loaded with household necessities
And stuff faced pork favourites
'Twas time to shed the caterpillar.
Entering gentlemen's cubicle
Jeans to try
My little lie
To re emerge
Mr Ben like
A full blown Mighty Hero
Of caped shock and awe
Civvies in a placky bag
A sudden snag
Sends us hurtling towards the tinned ravioli
'Holy Camoly'
A trolley wheel twister
Look out Sister
This is a job for…
She looks impressed
But I cannot rest
Until I've saved the day.
Taking immediate and firm control of the trolley
I turn it about
Steer us to the safety of the checkout
Where a titch of a lad
Tugs his Mother's coat for attention
Reality suspension
Wide eyed excitement and disbelief

He points and asks
'Where's your boots Superman?'
Taking me to task
My black shoed costume faux pas.
'I left my wet boots at the door of the store
So my Mom won't give me what for'!
Comes my desperate reply
Hope he'll turn a blind eye.
Face beaming
He shakes my hand and knew
Phew!
I'm the real deal
Man of Steel.
Vorsprung durch technik.

Sam

My boy, pride and joy
Now a man, real McCoy
My life continues on
I have a son

In the blink of an eye
He grows tall, touch the sky
His path has just begun
I have a son

Sweet youth passes by
He stands proud, so do I
Shoulders wide, he steps out
His world for the taking no doubt

But I'm here, should he need
My helping hand to succeed
His life continues on
I have a son

Keef

Keef, the face of corrugated iron
That's survived
A thousand battles and then some
With his mischievous self
The eyes say it all
By the glintful, sinful
A whorehouse grin
To incite
A Blusher's nightmare
He fills the gap
The mitts say it all
Handling shivs, pink slits and punks
Spliffs of Kingston sunshine
And six strings
With equal grace
Throwing away shapes
That lesser mortals might cling to
Like life itself
Those gnarled dukes
Dogs would love
To chew upon then bury
Though through dexterity, longevity
Blues, Booze and paid Dues
They, have buried the dogs
His guitar says it all
It's only Rock n Roll
But I like it

Watler Caine

Watler Caine, Le Petomane
His tuneful anus aimed to please
His stage of choice, the public bar
With trousers dropped about the knees

When plied with drink, it helped his stink
He pushed out farts upon request
His party piece 'The Birdy Song'
Until said birdy shat it's nest

Ten pints of stout came pouring out
The follow through a shock to see
Skating on a bed of slurry
Hard drinking men were seen to flee

Escorted from the premises
The liquid shit his trail of shame
His arsehole blew a last farewell
The pub would never be the same

When Watler Caine was laid to rest
'Twas said by all attending
They heard a haunting graveyard trump
Vaughn Williams 'Lark Ascending'

Peas

Mutha and her little sod
With covert code, a look, a nod
We laugh at things that folk find odd
We're two peas in a pod

Cricket

Chumberpud bowls a clump fodder
And Dilley hits an upper nip off to hard stump
Clump
Melting into the glove of wicket keeper Chadwick Whatsit
Today
In a way
Reminiscent of Alan Cox's sticky mitt of 2007
His weekend in Devon
And it's concluding grope in the slips.
I must say
After a long day of Veejay's short balls
Right up the bally gully what
I do feel this third test
Really is cricket at it's best.
Just a shame Beefy's a little out of sorts
His stomach aborts
Fifteen pints of Yorkshire's finest
Told everyone
To 'mid on'
'Mid off!' more like
On ya bike
Lovely bastard
Proper card
Now over to Tuffers for the twaddle banter.

Charlie's Head

Charlie
Wears his hair
With very little care indeed
Not on his head
But slightly above it
Elevation, Levitation?
Risen
Above its natural station
Like
Say
A hovercraft
A repulsion
Of magnetic fields perhaps?
No solidarity
More reversed polarity
In a halo
Of candy floss
In the manner of Arse Garfunkel
And his bridge over troubled Simon

Art Class

A Russian submarine Captain showed me some slides
And filled my eyes with all they had missed
He crammed my head with some much Wow
It remains
Forever open gaze
Whereupon a simple canvas
Great battles of thought
Fought
Then brought to me in weekly instalments
All the isms
Laid out for me to pick at
Gorge upon
Osmose
Each a call to arms
A philosophical gauntlet pitched
About the easel
I stare, I read, take up the brush
But which manifesto will guide my hey presto?
Whose truths will be mine?
Endless perceptions
Beautiful deceptions
And now
In mid conversation
I am lost in the lay of a shirt collar

Sunday Through The Roses

Ice cream smiles on little faces
Sauce and sprinkles, purple tongue
Hazy, lazy, days of sunshine
There we walk forever young

Mowers hum with cut grass perfume
Hedges trimmed from top to toe
Gleaming cars stand washed and rinsed
Their soapy suds in gutters flow

Slow cooked beef and mustard sinus
Flood the streets with fragrant trail
Great gravy boats of Yorkshire pud
From coast of roasters set their sail

Pigs in blankets lie with stuffing
All the herbs of Scarborough Fair
A lunch to munch, pork cracklin' crunch
Brigs snoozes in a comfy chair

Toddlers squeal out with excitement
Their flat foot slap a joy so pure
Puddles splashed down country lanes
Inhale the freshly spread manure

Canal sidewalks on tow path flat
A gentle stroll, a river ramble
Cycle bells ring 'step aside'
To sting of nettle, thorn and bramble

Village Greens, a Sunday league
The distant sound of sporting men
A cheer goes up, the crowd applaud
Our heroes of the now and then

A beery pint of heavy hopped
The glass upturned and double wasped
The tock of clock forever stopped
On Summer at it's best

Stop The Van

'Can we pull over love? I need the toilet
Stop the van, I want a piss'
All drive by, no hiding shy
Simply step down from the cab, bab
Up with skirt, down with knicker
Stand and deliver
No squat, just lean and piss with gusto
The formal bow of Japanese diplomacy
Or the cow of glorious pastures shat
Geisha, Gusher, pavement flusher
We all sit stare
In slack jawed hypnosis
Eyes drawn to the sluices, open torrent
Between her cheeks and thighs
Of a size
Fit to burst and now have
A view best plugged with Herriot's fist
Call Darrowby 385
She stands
In a puddle of her own making
And shimmy shakes
Chubby Checker like
The last of the drip drops
From whence Hubby gave her
'The Business'
Only three hours past
Knickers up, knitting out
'That's better lads'
And on we trundle

Sweet Little Betsy

Brenda has a baby Betsy
A dog like
Withered Yorkie thing
Rot on a string
In a word?
Absurd
But a small turd
Rolled in hair of matted grease
And finished with a pretty bow.
It squeaks and leaks
With relentless enthusiasm
And could
And should
Be sucked up by a vacuum cleaner
Have you seen her?
Dyson's happy misdemeanour.
But then
A lucky call
Poor old Brenda suffered a fall
The Gods?
Were kind
Placed Betsy beneath her behind
Cushioned the blow
Gateaux
RIP

Knit One Purl One

Brenda once knitted
And gifted to me
Three
Pickled onions

And a pair of 12th century socks.
Not a pair as in left and right
You understand?
More of an ambiguous
And an ambiguous extra long
Middle ages
All the rages
I'm really not pulling your poulaine!

Starman

From the bottom of The Seven Seas
To interstellar Starman
Stardom
The pure white cliffs of Mod
Smeared with the lippy of a Southern Belle
Androgynous, Epicene
This ambisexual athlete
The roasted toast of Warhol's New York
A dog with two of 'em
The all seeing eye
Of spellbinding light
Ronson helps to ignite
The red haired flames
Of intense genius
To be left in his ashes
Every generation
Has it's own Doctor
Who?
If only!

Food For Thought

Mr H
A fine gentleman of limited palate
Eats only toast, cake, chips and peas
Was once brought to his knees
By a pear
I swear!
Hospitalised by fruit.
Mrs H on the other hand
Slave to her pituitary gland
Eats anything and everything
The lot.
She eats and feasts without discernment, discrimination or bias
Fair play
And on the menu today?
The full Monty
The full nine yards.
The whole shooting match
Shebang
The whole kit and caboodle.
Noodle!
She eats her chow mien twice.
Coughing to the point of regurgitation
Her Mommy bird worms
Once tasted
Are not to be wasted.
Today's catch?
Back down the hatch
Bon Apetite

Iggy

From high school sweater
To Shamanic bloodletter
Osterberg's Lucky Jim
Wipes away the winning grin
Iguana sheds it's skin
And beaters and steps forth
In naked perfection
The Messiah antagonist
A human sacrifice unto himself
Sun God
Black Prince of Stooges
Blue print of Punk

Nan Joan

Nan Joan, she fed me fat
And gave me all I cared to take
Three suppers on a Friday night
Then licked the bowl and baked the cake

And as I grew, she fed my greed
And gave me all that I could taste
She even bought elastic slacks
To fit my forty eight inch waist

Shopping bags of lard and scratchings
So heavy they cut into hand
Ingredients for my funeral pyre
And with each bag the flames were fanned

And now she's gone, I waddle on
Her love remains for all to see
In fleshy folds of aches and pains
Who cares! Now what the fuck's for tea?

I Should Have Died There In Dubai

I should have died there in Dubai
I should have left without a fuss
With none to cry and wonder why
5,000 miles from any us

I lay and choked in bloodied bed
Like my hero's gone before
Too drunk to even roll my head
Alone behind locked hotel door

Hell was raised in sea of drink
Which now returned to set me free
With wrenching guts I start to drown
This seedy end, my destiny

The banging door crashed open wide
The Reaper foiled by saboteur
And from that moment on began
The years that almost never were

I should have died there in Dubai
I should have left without a fuss
But hope held out a loving hand
I came back home and made me 'us'

V For Victory – Me & Mom

So many bad days, broke, desperate, sad days
Made fun and it's making, all the more prized
With little or nothing, we created the special
The world of surreal, bizarre, improvised

The spirit that jinxed us, depresses and sinks us
Brings laughs all the louder, our will resolute
We tore up the rule book, the work and the school book
And gave and still give a two fingered salute

The Big Bear

I met a Big Bear in the market square
I sang him my songs, he gave me his smile
Those big city streets, all paved with busked pennies
From rag market to riches, we'd do in in style

All the bars and the pubs, the theatres and clubs
Travelled half 'round the world, had ourselves such a time
Some five-star affair, concerts held open air
Great festival stages, together we'd climb

The best I must mention, beyond comprehension
He made me a gift of the thing I most prized
An album of vinyl, my very own record
I held in my hands; all the dreams realised

Over thirty years on, with so much come and gone
Old me and old bear are still the same team
We sit down and smile, reminisce for a while
Then on with the show, as we plan our next dream

That Old Chestnut

Drink up folks and get your coats
It's time to go I fear
But sneaky wink has signalled drink
And two more rounds appear

A vodka here, a vodka there
Two rum and cokes with ice
'Whilst I'm serving, any beer?'
Yes, four pints would be nice

With huff and puff, some have enough
Look ready to explode
Though we'll depart, a mastered art
Brings one more for the road

When She Smiles

I just seem to smile when I look at her face
When she walks in a room, I'm in a warm place
I just seem to smile and relax for a while
I just seem to smile when she smiles

I just seem to know when I look in her eyes
Her eyes tell no lies, they don't wear a disguise
I just seem to know everything is just so
I just seem to smile when she smiles

Like the sun, she does shine, as she walks hand in mine
And we don't have a care
Light streaming through trees, tiger striped Summer breeze
I just stop and stare, for my world is right there

I just seem complete when she's by my side
Awash with her warmth, I'm swept with the tide
I just seem complete, there's no need to retreat
I just seem to smile when she smiles

My Hero

Twelve labours for the son of Zeus
A Minotaur stands in a maze
Jason steals the Golden Fleece
Odysseus ends the Cyclops' gaze

Upon my sea of dreams I float
And there the fabled Argo sails
The Sirens beckon with their song
All sprang from book, my bedtime tales

The largest conkers shook from tree
Tugged with rope tied 'round a stick
Once drilled and strung, the game is on
Baked or pickled, I take my pick

Forts and castles built with Lego
A battleground for tiny Knights
Meccano makes a working crane
For tabletop construction sites

Abandoned prams pulled from 'The Cut'
Old planks of wood saved just in case
The Phoenix rises as a go kart
Our street shall host a chariot race

Walking miles through fern and bracken
Climbing trees and hide and seek
Deep into the woods we'd play
My pine coned highlight of the week

Superman, Batman, Justice League
A shop where heroes fill the rack
A handful picked of DC's finest
Shared and swapped, read front to back

Some scraps of wood and chicken wire
With paper mache painted green
A tunnel passes through a mountain
Lichen trees to set the seen

Hornby locos shunt their cargo
Pullman's finest seat the rich
Signals flash and points are changed
When God like finger flicks the switch

Billiards, Snooker, Pool and Darts
No mercy, may the best man win
Ping Pong balls served hard and fast
All chopped and sliced for topmost spin

Seaside swims in Devon sunshine
Cricket and Football on the grass
In later years, weekends in Brugge
Fine Belgian beers to fill my glass

From Crazy golf to standing long jump
Pitch and Putt to jump the broom
Quizzes, puzzles, problem solving
Treasure hunts from room to room

Party games of raucous laughter
Tests of stamina, strength and skill
Endless hours spent supping ale
With no such thing as 'drank our fill'

A list that could go on forever
So much more that I could add
The greatest bond of man and boy
And all down to one man, my Dad

Life

At 5am I came home drunk
To find no wife, but just a note
I read and sobered in an instant
With thumping head, re zipped my coat

The taxi raced, then with much haste
I ran and reached hospital bed
And stood and stared at maker's name
Pushing out a little head

The screaming stopped, and there aloft
A child held high for all to see
'It's a baby' beamed my wife
Our tears of joy flowed openly

And there began a whole new world
A whole new life, a brand new start
And as he grew, our pride grew too
And boy, could he push out a fart

So now he stands at 6ft plus
The fine young man we knew he'd be
At 5 am he comes home drunk
The apple falls not far from tree x

The Forever Years

I came so close to losing you
And dipped my toe into the tears
The thought of all those forever years
Without you

The Rain in Spain Falls Mainly Over Here

They've seen their share of ups and downs
Those good old British seaside towns
Where bathers brave, but no one browns
In drizzle grey of day

Alfresco dining, bag of chips
The wind cuts cold, the shelter drips
I cannot feel my fingertips
My dog has blown away

And yet the whelks don't taste half bad
Those rocks I once climbed with my Dad
Striped deck chairs make my heart feel glad
And so I think I'll stay.

The New Recruit

I've been adopted of sorts, by a kind family.
In a time share of lovely times shared, I have them on long term loan
An exhibition of life, curated by my future wife
Her interactive gallery of love, care and nurturing
An art at which she excels
The family unit I had lost as a lad
And again, as a Dad
Now here
For me to get to know
And watch grow
Feel pride in their tomorrow
Not Christmas film schmaltz
Nor ad men's imagery
No white bath robes
No minted smiles
Sipping freshly squeezed orange juice without the bits
No
Not on your Nelly
Forget the telly
This is real and true
Perfectly imperfect
All the bits included

Shark Von Schtoop

I've seen him stand at many bars and on the house he'll drink his fill
Castles, manors, stately homes, he strolls straight in, no fee, no bill.

I've seen him wheeled onto a plane and carried off the other side
His wheelchair joke, a master stroke, he sat first class, all drinks
supplied

I've seen him drift by in The Rhine, his clothes tied up to make a float
I've seen him play the vacuum cleaner, atop a rich Norwegian's boat

I've seen him puff on fake cigars and has been asked to smoke outside
He also tokes a plastic carrot, a vegetable he smokes with pride

I've seen him stand in theatre wings and poke the drummer with a
pole
A pole of twenty foot or more, now tell me that's not Rock 'n' Roll

I've seen him piss over Adrian's wall, not on, but over, that's the thing
I've seen him dance on table tops and down a pint whilst yodelling

I've seen the love on children's faces, the grown ups too, are just the
same
I've seen him cast his happy spell, the rarest gift that few can claim

I've seen him make a person's day, a thousand fold and then some
more
I've seen him fill a place with joy, I heard their laughter, heard them
roar

He never fails to make me smile, I've seen him now for many years
We travel 'round and have it large, my dear ol' friend, The Baron,
CHEERS!

Have I Missed Something

'But what about the band?' you say
Ten thousand tales to curl the toes
From boys to men, we saw it all
How much of which should I disclose

Thirty years of raising hell
A book of laughs long over due
And there folks lies my next instalment
Please return for volume two!

On God's Watch

All the little children died
A million mothers mourn
And yet he worries who's had a wank
Or if you ate a prawn

The Robust Years

Robust mistrust, weasel word turds and Eton mess
Address, the burning issues
Swine porkers and Bullingdon waffle toffs
A spillage of gob farts and robust measures
Little treasures
Of spin scripted pap
On tap
Strong and stable, firm but fair
I spy a removed tie!
No need to doff your cap
A down to Earth man of the people
The pretence
Of 'I mean business' man graft and common sense
Hard hat for full effect
Affected, connected
Image projected
Like projectile vomit
Open white collar and rolled up cuffs
Here come the bluffs
Robust and dependable
Robust discussions and enquiries
Robust initiatives and approach
Robust systems in place
Robust optimisation and plans
At the grubby hands
Of the piss panted and saddle sore
Let me say this very clearly
I want to be clear on this
Let me be very clear on this
The Power Stance...
Ya saft Tit!

Cut Price Barbers

'Cut Price Barbers'
Stands, In his no man's land
As the to and fro of busy lives
Like sand
Pass through his fingers
Nobody lingers
Long, in his spidery shadow
Where, sat upon hairless linoleum
His empty chair
Awaits the unaware
Calling, Dead man walking
Longing for fresh blood and a bit off the top
No returning custom in this fellow's shop
Cut price barbers is a once only event
Repent
A fresh face of foolish mistake
Mine to make, I take the seat
Once caped, wrapped and trapped
He begins, strokes his chins
Downs scissors to offer guidance and council
'Well Sir, you see it's like this'…
Soapbox instruction on all that's amiss
Oracle, Categorical
The certainty of fools
'Let me explain something to you Sir'…
Sharing his acumen and understanding
How they faked the Moon landing
And the Hadron Collider will unlock the gates of hell
But what of the infidel? 9/11? Who goes to heaven?
God's will, the fuckin' contraceptive pill
And don't get him started on the cricket!
He reworks the cliches and makes them his own
'I never like to moan Sir, or speak ill of folk
Not like next door Sir, a horrible bloke
The kids of today think that hard works a joke
Asylum seekers, bloody sneakers
And all those on benefits'…

Droning, bemoaning, Gripes and banalities,
A vote for fatalities
'We should bring back hanging'.
He regains my attention
I eye him intently in the mirror
And find myself in full agreement.

Sidmouth Pier & Edward Lear

A night owl of old, who could have foretold
I'd chance on my pussy cat's face
A million to one, the same odds were on
That we'd come to our oh special place

The sunshine of sizzle, the cakes, lemon drizzle
Victoria sponge by the slice
Fine sandwich of crab, put the drinks on the tab
The posset is awfully nice

The gentlest of breeze, as we take our cream teas
And sit on our steps by the sea
All time seems to cease, in an ocean of peace
A time for just you and me

As we sit hand in hand, touch our feet to the sand
On a wave of contentment, we'll float
Let go of the rail, for it's time to set sail
On out beautiful pea green boat

Here then, together, together forever
And all through a meeting of chance
Let us sail on and on and when the sunlight has gone
By the light of the moon, we shall dance
We shall dance
By the light of the moon, we shall dance

Lockdown Madness

Winner takes all
Bog roll and pasta
A trolley mountain ringmaster
Sends in the clowns.
Grabby greedy
Trounce the needy
And all but the scraps of the selfish
Are left for the selfless and helpless
In a 'bag for life' of tough titty
And me, me, me.
Supermarket sweep
Swept
Nothing left
But the cabbages
And Crackerjack pencils,
Purged aisles and racks of empty
Like the make shift morgues
That await a thousand silent guests
Haunted
By the faint orange afterglow
Of the late Dale Winton

Losers Weepers

I walk the empty streets
But am not alone.
The watchers watch.
A nation in isolation
Abandoned
Frustration
At every turn
A double glazed stare
Gaunt
Lonely Despair
They line the windows
Like Dutch hookers custom
Pressed to the glass
Framed
A Gormleyesque tide
Of lonely soulless
Suckling upon maternal teats of tar
Puff and wheeze
Fear the warm Spring breeze
Carries with it
The poison of Wuhan
Drip spittle droplets
To take their breathe away
Finders
Keepers

Fit To Burst

A bubble must be six
You can't just pick and mix
But the trouble with a bubble
Is it cannot contain pricks

You'll Never Walk Alone

Detention suspension
As lowered guard and drawbridge
With some apprehension
We take the doorstep challenge
And step out into the light
Hermits unite
Right!
8 pm sharp
Make cheer and give thanks
Applaud those who
Tirelessly work on through
NHS
We love you.
Our heroes
Justly lauded
We turn
Let lockdown return
And then?
It begins
Who dares, wins
With truly captive audience
Every karaoke singer's big chance of glory.
'Testing, one two'
'This one's for you'
'Don't worry, be happy'
I hr 15 minutes last night.
The Bastard!

For Sanity's Sake

For sanity's sake
I made a clean break
From the drink and stink of my own self-worth.
My drinking cloak of bloke
Now a cumbersome yoke
Left hung up
Strung up
As I dropped my bravado
To the equally veneered floor.
And there stood
Raw
Unshelled
For near six weeks.
Without word or explanation,
Took vacation from libation
Staying clear of the pub
And those who might lead me into temptation.
But as I began to feel the benefits of being dry
My dear friend started to die
Made his last stand
Pint in hand
He faced his secret fate with lonely quiet dignity.
Absent without leave,
Without reprieve
I would not be privy to his illness or rapid end
And found out oh so very too late
My tardy tears of regret
Oh…
You can bet
I needed a drink

The Great Western Greats

Where have all the legends gone
Popped off clogs
Slip one by one
The Great Western greats
Ambled through pearly gates
To drink their fill in 'lock in' heaven.
The swillers and the shouters
The car park gladiators
Life's commentators
The great debaters
Cribbage Queens and limbo dancers
Masters of the pegboard
Domino Kings, all earned their wings
Arrive in 5s and 3s.
Bridget pulls pints and runs the gaff
Keeps out the riff raff
Those who earned their ticket on Earth can go to hell!
There goes the doorbell
And up goes a welcoming roar
Another good fine soul strolls through the door
Holds up a traffic cone
His makeshift megaphone and shouts up a beer
The room lets out a cheer
Raise their glasses and take a good long sup
Cheers Me Dears!

You couldn't make it up!

Absent Friends

Trevor didn't say goodbye on Tuesday afternoon
He didn't stop to shake my hand and say, 'I'll see you soon'
He didn't do his little wave, then go upon his way
There must have been a thousand thoughts, he didn't think to say

He didn't wear his linen suit, the one he kept for best
No Elvis Aaron Presley shirt sat proudly on his chest
He didn't wear his pocket watch with silver fob and chain
He didn't pack an ale or two, to sup upon the train

He didn't stroll up to the bar and order one last round
He didn't toast 'to absent friends', he didn't make a sound
Trevor didn't say goodbye that cold December's day
He just stood at the river's edge and quietly slipped away

Little Breeze

Hey little Breeze, you help the flowers grow
Hey little Breeze, you make the embers glow
Hey little Breeze, you warm my Summer's eve
Hey little Breeze, that pixie dust you leave

Hey little Breeze, with sunshine in your hair
Hey little Breeze, your sun shines everywhere
Hey little Breeze, you make the windmills twirl
Hey little Breeze, you're Grandad's girl

Goodbye Mr Chips

Barred for life from my local chip shop after rightly accusing the staff of thievery [on numerous occasions my order of meat samosas had been covertly substituted by their five pence cheaper vegetable counterparts], the consequential dip in profits now lead the manager to run out into the street as I pass and beg my return. Splendid.

Tottering through the chippy door
I find folk standing about like weeds
Sprung up in no discernible order.
I free fall
Bounce about them like a bagatelle ball
Before launching myself toward the empty counter.
'I'm next mate' pipes up some meandering clown.
'Then why not form a visible and decipherable queue?
Remember queues you cretinous fucktards?
You're all a shower of shit.'
I may have had a drink!
Right then!
Eyeing a trio of skewered elephant turds
I order the full mix up
Stuffed in a pitta of lard arse and lemon squeezy
If you pleasey
With all the sauces?
But of courses, plus an extra pot of Mr Naga's wipe and weep.
Four MEAT samosas, a battered todgerwhat and a cone of chips.
Any mayonnaise with that?
Certainly not.
Mayonnaise with chips!
The shock of Belgium '83
It'll never catch on in Blighty
Said me
Wrongly.
Whoops! I do the splits
A Northern Soul side step and scissors, then into a full body pop.
Ole!
Big John, sure plays a mean pinball.
Finally finding my sea legs, I continue to order

Two chilli wets
Three scallops with all the dollops
A forward roll
A shami, a shimi and a shish
With salad and trimmings, the full bastard
A duvet of nan and two popadopadipadoms
A portion of popcorn chicker lickers, and a shit with egg on it.

As supper is being cross referenced and bagged up
I fear I may have under ordered.
In a futile bid to conceal my gluttony I improvise an incoming call.
Yes, yes, I'm in the chip shop now. What would you like?
With phone pressed to my lug I relay the fictitious exchange –
'What's that you say? Yes, yes OK
A bag of pug knuckles
Four pieces of mucky fried cluck, breast not arse!
A chortle's worth of button fungus
One smoked wopperloy and a jar of edible Crustacea if you please?
Oh, and one of those large curried chunder balls and a pickle or three.
And that's me.

I lurch home hauling my bag of swag
Some I will eat, some I will wear and some I will decorate with.
All that beer and deep fried abandon
Now lies bubbling below the waist.
A right Umpah of Shinkel Shunkel Band and future shite housen.
I will finish the night by throwing a large jar of pickled beetroot
About my kitchen walls and ceiling
And then retire.
The following morning I return to the crime scene
Befuddled and bewildered.
What kind of devilment is this?
The drink. The damned drink. If only I could remember.

The hands of the Ripper have struck again.
May God forgive me.

Middle Aged Moment

I'm sitting in a perfect place
A perfect point in time and space
But happens to be our garden.
Nearby
My wife
Quietly bringing seeds to life
Her beautiful soul to see
In all the colours blooming
Bees and Bird song meet Jobim and Gilberto
Mingles melodious
A sun-bleached Samba of 'So Nice'
Glorious heavens of blue paradise
Seep through fragmented
Sweet scented
Golden chains of Laburnum
Twists of willow and silver birch
And there
I catch the eye of a fat man
Unexpected
In life's window reflected
A silver beard drips from his weak face
That miniscule moment of grace
Unrecognised.
I forget that he is Me
And this is now
Whatever now can be
And yet I see, he looks content
But all those years spent?
All came and went
But still
We share a smile
Nod in recognition
Of what we've done and all we've seen
And who we are and all we've been
And all those moments in between
And how we came to own this face
Now sitting in our perfect place.

The Telescope

The sea
Endlessly tripping over itself
Falling flat at my feet
The oceanic eternal circle of wonderment
So vast
The future and the past
Serves only to bring into view
My own horizon
My truth
All I know
And love
And ever will
When penny spent, the shutter will drop
Stop
The waves will still roll
The boats still sail
But not for my eyes
This beautiful holiday in the sun

It's been an absolute ball
I loved you all x

Author's Note

This project sprang from the COVID Lockdown of 2020-21, where, unable to visit family and friends, I decided to spend my 'time out' from The World reflecting on life and this wonderfully odd game of 'Snakes & Ladders' we all share.

Though my backside was to remain firmly parked in my garden studio, the contents of my head were free to roam. I became a time traveller of my years previous, able to stop at any of the shiny 'bits and bobs' that took my fancy, totally immerse myself and then return each night in time for tea. These reflections were sent out to family, in a hope to entertain, keep us chatting and most importantly look forward to enjoying together whatever was to become the new normal.

Arthur's Note

Not now Olive.

VERSE FROM APS PUBLICATIONS *(www.andrewsparke.com)*

Irrational Thoughts Random Rhymes (HR Beasley)
Random Word Trips (Lee Benson)
Close But Not Close Enough (Lee Benson)
Every Picture Hides A Friend (Lee Benson)
Failing To Be Serious (Lee Benson)
Got It Right (Lee Benson)
Jottings and Scribbles (Lee Benson)
Meandering With Intent (Lee Benson)
Backing Into The Limelight (Pete Crump)
Edging Out Of The Shadows (Pete Crump)
I've Landed (Empress P)
Inside Looking Out (Milton Godfrey)
Fluid Edges (David Hamilton)
Goddess Woman Butterfly Human (SC Lourie)
Reading Rites Writing Wrongs (Ian Meacheam)
Shining Light Dark Matters (Ian Meacheam)
Stone People Glass Houses (Ian Meacheam)
Word Bombs (Eddie Morton)
Dub Truth (Kokumo Noxid)
Pipe Dream (Kokumo Noxid)
Silent Songs Of Owen Parsnip (Angela Patmore)
The Highwayman, Pink Carnations and The Re-Allocated Coal Scuttle (Revie)
Drinkers Thinkers Outright Stinkers (Mark Skirving)
The Gathering (Malachi Smith)
Broken English (Andrew Sparke)
Fractured Time (Andrew Sparke)
Gutter Verse & The Baboon Concerto (Andrew Sparke)
Love & Levity (Andrew Sparke)
Refracted Light (Andrew Sparke)
Silent Melodies (Andrew Sparke)
Tea Among Kiwis (Andrew Sparke)
Tea and Symphony (Andrew Sparke)
Tequila & Me (Andrew Sparke)
The Mother Lode (Andrew Sparke)
Vital Nonsense (Andrew Sparke)
Wicked Virtue (Andrew Sparke)
Wild Verse (Andrew Sparke)
Still But Still Moving (Phil Thomson)
Riding The Top Deck (John Wright)
Artists 4 Syria (Various)
Walking The Edge (Various)

Printed in Poland
by Amazon Fulfillment
Poland Sp. z o.o., Wrocław
05 September 2021

a8891f81-a28d-4902-bb54-1acb0a85ca13R01